CREATIVE EDUCATION

GREEN BAY PACKERS

JOHN NICHOLS

Published by Creative Education
123 South Broad Street, Mankato, Minnesota 56001
Creative Education is an imprint of The Creative Company

Designed by Rita Marshall

Photos by: Allsport USA, AP/Wide World Photos, Bettmann/CORBIS,
SportsChrome

Library of Congress Cataloging-in-Publication Data

Nichols, John, 1966–
Green Bay Packers / by John Nichols.
p. cm. — (NFL today)
Summary: Traces the history of the Green Bay Packers from the team's
beginnings through 1999.
ISBN 1-58341-044-9

1. Green Bay Packers (Football team)—History—Juvenile literature. [1. Green
Bay Packers (Football team)—History. 2. Football—History.] I. Title. II. Series:
NFL today (Mankato, Minn.)

GV956.G7N53   2000
796.332'64'0977563—dc21   99-023741

First edition

9 8 7 6 5 4 3 2 1

Along the western shores of Lake Michigan, in the north-eastern section of Wisconsin, is a land of rushing rivers, pine forests, and abundant wildlife. In the 1630s, a French explorer and fur trader named Jean Nicolet first explored the area and established a frontier post along an inlet called Green Bay. This post grew into a thriving community that today is noted for its rustic beauty, tasty cheeses, and world-famous professional football team—the Green Bay Packers.

Pro football has been an important part of life in Green Bay since 1919. The Packers, one of the oldest franchises in the National Football League, have a long and exciting his-

Don Hutson (#14) with Curly Lambeau and Irv Comp.

tory. In addition to winning 12 world championships, they are the first and only NFL team to win three consecutive league titles, and they've done it twice. They were also the first Super Bowl champs, winning Super Bowls I and II under legendary coach Vince Lombardi.

Packer greats over the years—such as Curly Lambeau, Don Hutson, Bart Starr, Ray Nitschke, Willie Davis, Sterling Sharpe, Reggie White, and Brett Favre—have left their mark on pro football. They have also created a Packers tradition of excellence that has thrilled fans for more than 80 years.

Curly Lambeau helped the Packers outscore their opponents 565–12.

THE EARLY YEARS

In 1919, Earl "Curly" Lambeau, one of pro football's pioneers, worked for a meat-packing company in Green Bay. He asked his boss at the Indian Packing Company to put up the $500 needed for equipment and uniforms to start up a new team. The boss agreed, and Lambeau named the team the "Packers" in gratitude.

The equipment was simple in those early days. Players wore leather helmets without face guards and few, if any, pads. Most played both offense and defense since the team roster was usually less than 20 men. Salaries were even more modest than the equipment. At the end of the Packers' first season, the players split the profits evenly—$16.75 per man.

Lambeau was a strict disciplinarian who knew how to win. He played quarterback and directed the offense, guiding his team to a 10–1 record in 1919. During one early game, three Green Bay running backs were carried from the field with broken bones. Out of necessity, Lambeau began

Defensive end Vonnie Holliday.

*Fullback Clarke
Hinkle led Green
Bay in rushing
yards (384) for the
third straight year.*

calling passing plays, and the Packers won 33–0. "That's when I learned the value of the forward pass," he recalled. Lambeau quarterbacked the team for 10 seasons. Then, in 1929, he retired to concentrate solely on coaching the Packers for the next 20 years.

The early Packers, with their combined land and air attacks, soon became a powerhouse in the new National Football League and were champions in 1929, 1930, and 1931 with a combined record of 34–5–2. The team's stars included four future Hall-of-Famers—linemen Cal Hubbard and Mike Michalske, and backs Johnny (Blood) McNally and Clarke Hinkle. But the best was yet to come.

In 1935, a young receiver from Pine Bluff, Arkansas, named Don Hutson joined the Packers and helped Curly Lambeau turn the passing game into an art form. With his speed and grace, Hutson soon earned the nickname "the Alabama Antelope."

Hutson made his mark in the league right away. In his first play from scrimmage, he grabbed an 83-yard touchdown strike from quarterback Arnie Herber. It was the first of 488 catches Hutson would make and the first of 99 touchdowns he would score in his record-breaking career.

Hutson's record of 99 touchdown pass receptions went unchallenged for 44 years until Seattle's Steve Largent surpassed it in 1989. Several of Hutson's other benchmarks still stand today, including most seasons leading the league in touchdown catches (nine) and most seasons leading the league in pass receptions (eight). Hutson was the terror of the NFL and the force behind the Packers' next three league championships in 1936, 1939, and 1944.

When Hutson retired after the 1945 season and Lambeau called it quits in 1949, the first great football era in Green Bay ended. The team hit rock bottom during the 1958 season, finishing with a 1–10–1 record, the worst in franchise history. It was time for a change.

COACH LOMBARDI

The biggest change was the addition of a new head coach: Vince Lombardi, a 45-year-old former assistant with the New York Giants. Lombardi, known to most as simply "Coach," insisted on an unusually long five-year contract with the Packers, promising to create a winner during that period. He did much more than that. During Lombardi's first five years, the Packers not only posted winning records each year, they made the playoffs four times and captured the NFL championship twice. Then, in the next four years, Lombardi led the team to three more league titles.

When Lombardi arrived in Green Bay in 1959, he told his players, "I have never been on a losing team, gentlemen, and I do not intend to start now!" The players were clearly impressed, and the club rebounded from its previous season to post a winning 7–5 record in 1959.

Lombardi was a taskmaster, but he was also able to enjoy a laugh with his players. Max McGee, a star receiver for Green Bay, remembered: "I could make him laugh, and I know he liked me because of it. He'd back himself into an emotional corner, and I would get him out of it. After we won a game 6–3 on two field goals, he was furious. He told us to forget everything he'd taught us, to scrap it all, that we

1 9 5 9

Vince Lombardi began his Hall of Fame career as Green Bay's coach.

The NFL's all-time sacks leader, Reggie White.

Hard-charging fullback Jim Taylor.

were going back to basics. He reached down and picked up a football and said, with a sarcastic grin all over his face, 'This is a football.' And I said, 'Slow it down a little, Coach. You're going too fast.'"

Lombardi ran the team with a strong hand from the sidelines, but he also had a coach on the field: quarterback Bart Starr. Starr had been drafted out of the University of Alabama in 1956 and never showed much promise until Lombardi arrived in Green Bay and made him a starter. Starr rewarded Lombardi's faith in him by setting dozens of NFL records before his retirement in 1971. He completed a higher percentage of passes than any previous quarterback in NFL history (57.4 percent); led the league in passing in 1962, 1964, and 1966; and was named the Most Valuable Player in both Super Bowls I and II. In the eight seasons between 1960 and 1967, Starrs's Packers captured five NFL championships.

But there were many other heroes during the Lombardi era: running backs Jim Taylor and Paul Hornung, offensive linemen Forrest Gregg and Jim Ringo, and defensive standouts Ray Nitschke, Willie Davis, Willie Wood, and Herb Adderley. Two other unsung heroes were offensive guards Jerry Kramer and Fred "Fuzzy" Thurston, whose blocks often sprung Green Bay running backs for long gains. Kramer made one of the most famous blocks in NFL history during a game that is usually referred to as the "Ice Bowl."

It was December 31, 1967, and the Dallas Cowboys were playing in Green Bay's outdoor stadium for the NFL championship. The temperature was a bitter minus 13 degrees, and the warm-weather Cowboys were wearing gloves and frowns as icy winds whipped across the field. Coach Lombardi told his gloveless Packers players, "You've got to be bigger than the weather to be a winner."

Green Bay found itself in a tough struggle with both the elements and the Cowboys. Late in the game, with the sun setting, the Packers had one final chance to overcome a 17–14 Dallas lead. Starting from its own 31-yard line, Green Bay drove the length of the field. On third down, with the ball inside the Dallas one-yard line and only 16 seconds remaining, Lombardi had a big decision to make. Should the Packers go for the winning touchdown and risk running out of time if they failed, or kick a short field goal to tie the game and force sudden-death overtime?

1 9 6 4

Running back Paul Hornung also served as Green Bay's kicker, scoring 107 points.

"I thought of the fans," Lombardi later said. "I couldn't stand to think of them sitting in those cold stands during overtime." He and Starr agreed that the best plan was a quarterback sneak.

Starr described the play: "We had noticed earlier that Jethro Pugh, the Cowboys' tackle on the left side, charged too high on goal-line situations. So we knew a quarterback sneak would work. Jerry Kramer was confident he could block Pugh."

When the pile of bodies was separated, Starr and Kramer were both across the goal line, and the Packers had won the game and the NFL title 21–17.

But the season was not yet over for the Packers. For the second straight year, they would take on the champion of the American Football League (AFL) in the Super Bowl. A year earlier, Green Bay had won Super Bowl I, 35–10, over the Kansas City Chiefs. Now the team would have a chance to defend its title against the Oakland Raiders.

Jim Taylor brought his Packers career to a close after gaining a team-record 8,207 yards.

There was added pressure on the Green Bay players during Super Bowl II. Rumors had spread that "Coach" planned to retire after the game. Lombardi gave a stirring pregame pep talk, and his players responded with an impressive 33–14 win. Forrest Gregg and Jerry Kramer carried Lombardi from the field on their shoulders. "This is the best way to leave a football field," said Lombardi.

The following year, Lombardi served as Green Bay general manager only. He quickly became bored off the field, however, and began looking for a new coaching challenge. A year later, Lombardi took over as coach of the Washington Redskins, a team as bad as the Packers had been before he arrived in Green Bay. He was turning that club around, too, when he became ill with cancer and died. The entire nation mourned the loss of a truly great man, but nowhere was there more grief than in Green Bay.

THE POST-LOMBARDI ERA

Following Vince Lombardi's retirement, the Packers struggled to recapture their dominant ways, making the playoffs only once during the next 14 years and finishing above .500 only three times. New players and coaches came and went—nothing seemed to make a difference as the Packers dwelled near the bottom of the division.

In an effort to revive the old Packers tradition, the club's owners brought in Bart Starr as head coach in 1975. Starr, like Lombardi, found a team with potential. But unlike Lombardi, Starr was never able to build a consistent winner in Green Bay.

Legendary quarterback Bart Starr.

Hall of Fame linebacker Ray Nitschke.

Starr's greatest success came in developing a recharged Packers passing attack in the early 1980s. With Lynn Dickey as quarterback and James Lofton and John Jefferson at the wide receiver positions, the Packers became an aerial powerhouse. Unfortunately, the club lacked defensive muscle, often giving up 30 or more points a game to the opposition.

In 1982, Starr's team finally reached playoff territory. Green Bay posted a 5–3–1 mark in the strike-shortened season and earned a postseason berth for the first time in 11 years.

In the Wild Card playoff game, Dickey's passing spearheaded a 41–16 romp over the St. Louis Cardinals. The win set up a playoff confrontation with the Dallas Cowboys for the first time since the Ice Bowl. This time the Cowboys won, 37–26.

Green Bay fans were expecting great things from the Packers in 1983. What they received was heart-stopping drama. Four games were decided in overtime—an NFL record. Five others were won or lost by four points or less.

The divisional championship that season hinged on Green Bay's last game against the Chicago Bears. If the Packers won, they would capture the championship and make the playoffs for a second straight year. If they lost, their season would be over. Late in the game, Green Bay was up 21–20, but Bears kicker Bob Thomas booted a last-second field goal through the uprights, sealing the Packers' fate and Bart Starr's as well. A few weeks later, he was fired as head coach and replaced by his former teammate Forrest Gregg.

Vince Lombardi had once called Gregg "the finest player I ever coached." Now Packers fans counted on him to return the team to its former glory.

1 9 7 5

John Brockington led Green Bay in rushing for the fifth consecutive season.

Like Lombardi, Brett Favre was a natural leader (pages 18-19).

Gregg decided to emphasize defense over offense, adding such players as defensive end Robert Brown, linebacker Tim Harris, and defensive back Mark Murphy. Unfortunately, the team never became a winner. Following a miserable 5–9–1 campaign in 1987, Gregg resigned, and the Packers found themselves looking for new leadership again.

1 9 8 9

Quarterback Don Majkowski led the Packers to a string of come-from-behind victories.

A LITTLE GREEN BAY MAJIK

After Gregg's departure, Green Bay management decided to look outside the Packers family for a new head coach. They selected Cleveland Browns offensive coordinator Lindy Infante, who came to Wisconsin full of optimism. "I feel good about where we're going," he told fans. "I feel good about the majority of people who are going to get us there." Infante based much of his optimism on the presence of quarterback Don Majkowski, a late-round draft pick in 1987 out of the University of Virginia.

Majkowski, who had surprised many people by winning the starting role in his rookie year, really came into his own after Infante arrived. The new coach encouraged Majkowski to increase his knowledge of football strategy. "I want you to be a manipulator, not a gunslinger," Infante told him. Majkowski listened and began spending more time studying game films. Although his efforts made him a wiser player, it was his ability to scramble and turn potentially disastrous situations into long gains that earned him the nickname "Majik" and the adoration of the fans.

Majik's late-game heroics during the 1989 season helped transform Green Bay from a 4–12 team in 1988 to a 10–6 contender. Majik and second-year wide receiver Sterling Sharpe became the most potent passing combo in the league. Majkowski set club records with 599 attempts and 353 completions, and Sharpe led the NFL with 90 catches. Both players earned Pro Bowl berths along with linebacker Tim Harris, who topped all NFC defenders with an impressive 19.5 sacks.

Green Bay fans were certain that a new "golden age" was starting. In addition to Majkowski and Sharpe, the Packers had a third offensive star in Pro-Bowl running back Brent Fullwood. Green Bay's defense, meanwhile, boasted a talented secondary that included Mark Murphy, Chuck Cecil, and new arrival LeRoy Butler.

1 9 9 0

Safety Mark Murphy was one of three Packers defensive backs to intercept three passes.

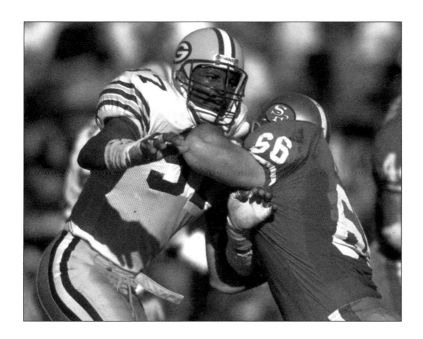

Ferocious linebacker Tim Harris.

Receiver Sterling Sharpe combined great speed and power.

Unfortunately, injuries to both Majkowski and Sharpe caused the Pack to fall to 6–10 in 1990 and 4–12 in 1991. Lindy Infante was dismissed, and it was time for Green Bay to start all over again.

THE HOLMGREN ERA

Head coach Mike Holmgren led the Packers back to respectability with a 9–7 record.

Step one in the Packers' rebuilding effort involved finding the right coach. Green Bay management soon recruited 49ers offensive coordinator Mike Holmgren to become the team's new head man.

Holmgren was widely known for his ability to develop young quarterbacks. He had already helped San Francisco's Steve Young become the top-rated passer in NFL history, and he hoped to duplicate this feat with another young signal-caller, Brett Favre, whom the Packers had obtained in a trade with Atlanta before the 1992 season.

Favre had sat on the Falcons' bench for most of the 1991 season, and he was thrilled to join Holmgren in Green Bay. Leading a revitalized Packers offense, Favre completed 302 passes for more than 3,200 yards in 1992. An NFL-record 108 of those passes went to Sterling Sharpe, now fully recovered from his injuries. Rookie halfback Edgar Bennett added another dimension to the Packers' attack as both a rusher and receiver, while linebackers Tony Bennett and Bryce Paup keyed a greatly improved defense.

The team's new stars helped the Packers win six of their last seven games to finish at 9–7. Green Bay would have made the playoffs but for a season finale loss to Minnesota.

End Reggie White made 98 tackles and an NFC-best 13 sacks.

The next year, the Pack was truly back. Favre and Sharpe combined for 112 passes, surpassing their own NFL record. Green Bay also added another major weapon: future Hall of Fame defensive end Reggie White, who signed as a free agent before the 1993 season. White, the NFL's career quarterback sack leader, keyed a defense that gave up more than 30 points only twice all season. "I don't think there has ever been a guy at his position with Reggie White's combination of size, speed, and strength," said one opposing coach.

Green Bay finished at 9–7 for the second straight year and made the playoffs for the first time since 1982. But the Packers weren't ready to stop there.

In the Wild Card contest against the Detroit Lions, Favre led the Packers offense on an exciting last-minute drive down the field. With 55 seconds to go and Detroit up 24–21, Green Bay had the ball on the Lions' 40-yard line. On the next play, Favre spotted Sharpe all alone in the end zone and threw a dangerous pass across his body more than 60 yards. Sharpe grabbed it for the winning score.

Even though the Packers lost 27–17 to the Dallas Cowboys the following week, most Green Bay fans believed that the team's luck was finally changing. A third straight winning season in 1994 and another Wild Card playoff win against the Lions convinced even more people. There was, however, one sad note. Sterling Sharpe, on his way to another record-breaking year, suffered a neck injury that ended his playing career. Losing Sharpe was a blow to the Green Bay offense, but the emergence of speedy receiver Robert Brooks helped keep the Green Bay passing attack among the best in the league.

Before the 1995 season, Coach Holmgren told reporters, "Brett Favre is the key. Our football team will almost automatically take the next step with him." Favre took giant steps in 1995, and so did the Packers. Favre topped the NFL with 359 completions for 4,413 yards and 38 touchdowns, winning the league's Most Valuable Player award. His passing also opened up the Green Bay running game, and Edgar Bennett became the team's first 1,000-yard rusher since Terdell Middleton in 1978.

1 9 9 5

Robert Brooks led Green Bay in receiving yards (1,497) and touchdowns (13).

Green Bay fans got into the act, too. Packers players, after crossing the end zone, would often hurl themselves into the stands—a celebration dubbed the "Lambeau Leap"—to share the joyous moment with the crowd.

Following playoff victories over the Atlanta Falcons and the defending Super Bowl champion San Francisco 49ers, the Packers found themselves facing off against the Dallas Cowboys for the NFC title. Although Packers fans were treated to a great game between the two football heavyweights, their team came up short as the Cowboys rallied for two fourth-quarter touchdowns to win 38–27.

The loss was painful, but there was even more distressing news on the way. After the season, Favre publicly announced that he was addicted to drugs. During the season, he had become hooked on the painkillers he took to fight off various aches and pains.

But Packers fans didn't have anything to worry about. After getting treatment over the summer, Favre was in top form once again in 1996, and one opponent after another fell as the Packers rolled to a 13–3 record. Favre's 39 touchdown passes earned him a second straight MVP trophy, and

Dorsey Levens powered Green Bay's ground attack (pages 26-27).

Pro-Bowl tight end Mark Chmura excelled at blocking and caught six scoring passes.

a stingy Green Bay defense gave up 20 or more points in only four games. All the pieces were in place for a run at the championship.

After running over the San Francisco 49ers and Carolina Panthers in the playoffs, the Packers squared off against the New England Patriots in Super Bowl XXXI. The experts had said all year that the Packers were the best team in the league, and they were right. A 35–21 win brought the championship trophy back to Green Bay for the first time since 1967. The only thing elated Packers fans loved more than the victory was Green Bay's odds to repeat as champs the following season.

The Packers' offensive machine came out firing on all cylinders again in 1997. Favre threw 35 touchdowns on his way to a share of an NFL-record third straight MVP trophy; young running back Dorsey Levens charged for 1,435 yards; and receivers Robert Brooks and Antonio Freeman formed a dangerous duo with more than 1,000 receiving yards apiece. After one impressive Packers win, fullback William Henderson summed up what most of the football world already believed. "When we have all our weapons in use like we did today, and Brett is rolling, it's going to be hard for anyone to stop us."

After cruising through the regular season and playoffs, the Packers met the Denver Broncos in the Super Bowl. Although Green Bay was heavily favored, the John Elway-led Broncos won Super Bowl XXXII, 31–24, in one of the most exciting championship games ever.

The Packers mounted another championship drive in 1998, but injuries slowed the team. After putting together an

11–5 record, the Packers' Super Bowl run was halted by a 30–27 playoff loss to the San Francisco 49ers.

Green Bay soon suffered another loss when Reggie White announced his retirement, stepping down after notching an NFL-record 192.5 quarterback sacks in 14 seasons. To make matters worse, the Packers also lost their head coach when Mike Holmgren left Green Bay to become the coach and general manager of the Seattle Seahawks. "There is a time for everybody to move on and find new challenges," Holmgren said, "and now the time is mine."

Wide receiver Bill Schroeder caught 74 passes for 1,051 total yards.

THE TRADITION CONTINUES

With the loss of Holmgren and White, the Packers needed to find new leaders—both on the field and on the sidelines—to carry on the franchise's success. Green Bay filled its coaching void by hiring former Philadelphia Eagles head coach Ray Rhodes. The fiery Rhodes had been a coaching assistant in San Francisco, a defensive coordinator in Green Bay, and a head coach in Philadelphia before coming back to the Packers franchise.

Fortunately for Green Bay fans, the Packers also had a young star ready to take the place of the great Reggie White. Vonnie Holliday, a 6-foot-5 and 300-pound defensive end, had been Green Bay's first-round pick in the 1998 NFL draft. "This guy's something else," said Packers center Frank Winters after trying to block Holliday in practice. "He's as strong as an ox and quick, too. I'm glad he's with us."

Helping Holliday anchor the Packers' defense was All-Pro safety LeRoy Butler and talented young cornerback Mike

Brett Favre was named NFL MVP in 1995, 1996, and 1997.

Defensive leader LeRoy Butler.

Big tackle Russell Maryland hoped to solidify the Packers' run defense.

McKenzie. Meanwhile, on offense, the Packers counted again on three-time league MVP Brett Favre to make life miserable for opposing defenses. The star quarterback continued to have plenty of weapons at his disposal, including versatile running back Dorsey Levens and speedy receiver Antonio Freeman.

Unfortunately, 1999 turned out to be one of Green Bay's worst seasons in years. Brett Favre suffered an injury to his right thumb and had trouble gripping the ball for much of the season. The scrappy quarterback toughed it out and played every game, but his passes did not have the same zip or accuracy. Favre passed for 22 touchdowns but also misfired for 23 interceptions.

With their quarterback hobbled, the Packers sputtered to an 8–8 finish and missed the playoffs for the first time since 1992. Packers management, disappointed in the team's performance, decided to fire Ray Rhodes. They soon replaced him with former Packers assistant coach Mike Sherman, who had been on Holmgren's coaching staff and knew the team's playbook well. "I know these guys, and they know what I'm all about," said the new coach. "I think with a lot of hard work this team can be great again."

Fans have no doubt that today's Packers are capable of adding to the championship legacy of the historic franchise. With the leadership of Brett Favre and the addition of such players as former Raiders defensive tackle Russell Maryland, the day may soon come when Green Bay is known as "Title-town" once again.